Daily Inspirations

Compressed Philosophy And Distilled

Wisdom To Make You Think

What the papers say about Dr Vernon Coleman and his books

❖ '... no thinking person can ignore him. This is why he has been for over 20 years one of the world's leading advocates on human and animal rights in relation to health. Long may it continue!' THE ECOLOGIST

❖ 'Despite my own medical training and knowledge of nature's devices, Dr Coleman made me think again.' BBC WORLD SERVICES

❖ 'Superstar!' INDEPENDENT ON SUNDAY

❖ 'Coleman has been a thorn in the side of the medical establishment for the past quarter of a century.' HERE'S HEALTH

❖ '...his future as king of the media docs is assured.' THE INDEPENDENT

❖ 'Vernon Coleman writes brilliant books.' THE GOOD BOOK GUIDE

❖ 'The revered guru of medicine.' NURSING TIMES

❖ 'Perhaps the best known health writer in the world today.' THE THERAPIST

❖ 'The Lone Ranger, Robin Hood and the Equalizer rolled into one.' EVENING TIMES

❖ 'Britian's leading medical author.' THE DAILY STAR

❖ 'Brilliant.' THE PEOPLE

❖ 'The patient's champion.' BIRMINGHAM POST

❖ 'The medical expert you can't ignore.' SUNDAY INDEPENDENT

❖ 'Dr Coleman writes with more sense than bias.' DAILY EXPRESS

What a few of Dr Coleman's readers have to say:

❖ 'Your willingness to say exactly what you think is a refreshing change.' P.H., HANTS

❖ 'I admire your forthright and refreshingly honest way of expressing your views and opinions ... bless you for being a light in the eternal darkness.' B.O., DURHAM

❖ 'If only more people in the medical profession and this government were like you it would be a much nicer world.' G.W., HANTS

❖ 'My deep appreciation for your great courage and integrity over the years.' J.T., U.S.A.

❖ 'I have never before had the patience to sit down and read a book but once I started your book a few weeks ago I was riveted.' S.K., BIRMINGHAM

❖ 'I admire your direct approach and philosophy in respect of general health.' A.W., DURHAM

❖ 'It's lovely to have someone who cares about people as you do. You tell us such a lot of things that we are afraid to ask our own doctors.' K.C., NEWCASTLE

❖ 'I would like to thank you for telling us the truth' R.K., KENT

❖ 'I feel I must write and congratulate you ... your no-nonsense attitude, teamed with plain common sense makes a refreshing change ... please keep up the good work.' L.B., LEICS

❖ 'Thanks over and over again – good health always to you as you are fighting for a good cause in life – for the sick.' E.H., CLEVELAND

❖ 'I only wish to God that we had a few such as your good self in parliament, then maybe our standard of life would possibly be better.' H.H., SOMERSET

❖ 'I greatly admire your no nonsense approach to things and your acting as champion of the people.' L.L., CORNWALL

❖ 'I have now read and studied all your excellent books and have enjoyed and benefited from them immensely.' B.B., DORSET

❖ 'Your no nonsense approach to the medical profession is a tonic.' C.S., TYNE & WEAR

❖ 'I admire your courage to speak out for what you believe to be the truth.' E.C., NORTHANTS

❖ 'May I say that I think you have done a real service to all those who have the sense and patience to study your books.' B.A., HAMPSHIRE

❖ 'I've just read Bodypower and Food for Thought. They will now go onto my bookshelf to be re-read many times in the future.' G.G., BUCKS

Other books by Vernon Coleman

The Medicine Men (1975)
Paper Doctors (1976)
Everything You Want To Know About Ageing (1976)
Stress Control (1978)
The Home Pharmacy (1980)
Aspirin or Ambulance (1980)
Face Values (1981)
Guilt (1982)
The Good Medicine Guide (1982)
Stress And Your Stomach (1983)
Bodypower (1983)
An A to Z Of Women's Problems (1984)
Bodysense (1984)
Taking Care Of Your Skin (1984)
A Guide to Child Health (1984)
Life Without Tranquillisers (1985)
Diabetes (1985)
Arthritis (1985)
Eczema and Dermatitis (1985)
The Story Of Medicine (1985, 1998)
Natural Pain Control (1986)
Mindpower (1986)
Addicts and Addictions (1986)
Dr Vernon Coleman's Guide To Alternative Medicine (1988)
Stress Management Techniques (1988)
Overcoming Stress (1988)
Know Yourself (1988)
The Health Scandal (1988)
The 20 Minute Health Check (1989)
Sex For Everyone (1989)
Mind Over Body (1989)
Eat Green Lose Weight (1990)
Why Animal Experiments Must Stop (1991)
The Drugs Myth (1992)
Why Doctors Do More Harm Than Good (1993)
Stress and Relaxation (1993)
Complete Guide To Sex (1993)
How to Conquer Backache (1993)
How to Conquer Arthritis (1993)

Betrayal of Trust (1994)
Know Your Drugs (1994, 1997)
Food for Thought (1994)
The Traditional Home Doctor (1994)
I Hope Your Penis Shrivels Up (1994)
People Watching (1995)
Relief from IBS (1995)
The Parent's Handbook (1995)
Oral Sex: Bad Taste And Hard To Swallow? (1995)
Why Is Pubic Hair Curly? (1995)
Men in Dresses (1996)
Power over Cancer (1996)
Crossdressing (1996)
How To Get The Best Out Of Prescription Drugs (1996)
How To Get The Best Out of Alternative Medicine (1996)
How To Conquer Arthritis (1996)
High Blood Pressure (1996)
How To Stop Your Doctor Killing You (1996)
How To Overcome Toxic Stress (1990,1996,2000)
Fighting For Animals (1996)
Alice and Other Friends (1996)
Dr Coleman's Fast Action Health Secrets (1997)
Dr Vernon Coleman's Guide to Vitamins and Minerals (1997)
Spiritpower (1997)
Other People's Problems (1998)
How To Publish Your Own Book (1999)
How To Relax and Overcome Stress (1999)
Animal Rights – Human Wrongs (1999)
Superbody (1999)
The 101 Sexiest, Craziest, Most Outrageous Agony Column Questions
    (and Answers) of All Time (1999)
Strange But True (2000)
Food For Thought [revised edition] (2000)
The Complete Guide To Life (2000)

reports

Prostate Trouble (2000)
Vitamins and Minerals (2000)
How To Campaign (2000)
Genetic Engineering (2000)
Osteoporosis (2000)

Vaccines (2000)
Alternative Medicine (2000)

novels

The Village Cricket Tour (1990)
The Man Who Inherited a Golf Course (1995)
The Bilbury Chronicles (1992)
Bilbury Grange (1993)
Mrs Caldicot's Cabbage War (1993)
Bilbury Revels (1994)
Deadline (1994)
Bilbury Country (1996)
Second Innings (1999)
Around the Wicket (2000)

short stories

Bilbury Pie (1995)

on cricket

Thomas Winsden's Cricketing Almanack (1983)
Diary Of A Cricket Lover (1984)

as Edward Vernon

Practice Makes Perfect (1977)
Practise What You Preach (1978)
Getting Into Practice (1979)
Aphrodisiacs – An Owner's Manual (1983)
Aphrodisiacs – An Owner's Manual (Turbo Edition) (1984)
The Complete Guide To Life (1984)

as Marc Charbonnier

Tunnel (novel 1980)

with Dr Alan C Turin

No More Headaches (1981)

with Alice

Alice's Diary (1989)
Alice's Adventures (1992)

Daily Inspirations

Compressed Philosophy And Distilled

Wisdom To Make You Think

Vernon Coleman

BLUE
BOOKS

Published by Blue Books, Publishing House, Trinity Place, Barnstaple, Devon, EX32 9HJ, England.

ISBN: 1 899726 25 X

A catalogue record for this book is available from the British Library.

Printed by Antony Rowe Limited, Wiltshire

Dedicated to Donna Antoinette, the Welsh Princess

FOREWORD

When I was young I thought it was sacriligeous to mark the books I read. And then, a few decades ago, I made a faint pencil mark in a paperback by P.G. Wodehouse in order to help me re-find a passage I liked a lot.

It was a step on a slippery slope. Since then I haven't looked back. These days I never read a book (unless it's a rare first edition) without a pen or a pencil in my hand. Every time I come across something which makes me think I put a mark in the margin. Sometimes, if the book is borrowed, I scribble down the quotation on a slip of paper.

This is how I put this book together.

Like most writers I have a fine collection of books of quotations. But this book is a taste from my personal collection of quotes – a collection which is derived first hand from some of my favourite authors and many of my favourite books.

Most of these quotes really made me think and many of them are funny. (That doesn't mean that some of the funny ones aren't also provocative.)

With a cavalier and comprehensive disregard for the conventions of false modesty I have included quotes from many of my own books in this collection.

Vernon Coleman, Devon 2000

1st January

'It is not enough to be busy. The question is: "What are you busy about"?'

Henry David Thoreau

• •

2nd January

'Never apologise for showing feeling, my friend. Remember that when you do, you apologise for truth.'

Benjamin Disraeli

• •

3rd January

'"Neutral", "objective", "fair" and "responsible" are qualities which we are taught to admire. But, in truth, these are the qualities of the weak spirited and the passionless. Name me one great man who was ever "fair". Name me a social, technical or artistic advance produced by a "bland" man.'

Vernon Coleman

• •

4th January

'Truth is on the march and nothing will stop it.'

Emile Zola

• •

5th January

'It is from nature that the disease arises and from nature comes the cure, not from the physician.'

Paracelsus

• •

6th January

'What a different story men would have to tell if only they would adopt a definite purpose, and stand by that purpose until it had time to become an all-consuming obsession.'

Napoleon Hill

• •

7th January

'In most people's lives the good luck and the bad luck cancel one another out – and the trick is to try and take the greatest possible advantage of all the good luck so that you can ride all the bad luck.'

Vernon Coleman

• •

8th January

'Believe nothing, no matter where you read it, or who said it! No matter if I have said it, unless it agrees with your own reason and with your own common sense.'

Buddha

• •

9th January

'Of course we can splice genes. But can we *not* splice genes?'

Jean Paul Sartre

. . . .

10th January

'If I were confined to a corner of a garret all my days, like a spider, the world would be just as large to me while I had my thoughts about me.'

Henry David Thoreau

. . . .

11th January

'A small bacterium weighs as little as 0.00000000001 gram. A blue whale weighs about 100,000,000 grams. Yet a bacterium can kill a whale.'

Dr Bernard Dixon

. . . .

12th January

'We make walls, floor, roof, doors and windows for a room. But it is the empty space within that makes the room liveable. Thus, while the tangible have advantages it is the intangible that makes it useful.'

Tao Te Jing by Lao Tsu

. . . .

13th January

'There are more old drunkards than old doctors.'

Benjamin Franklin

● ●

14th January

'The ruler must not display his weapons if he is to survive long.'

Tao Te Jing by Lao Tsu

● ●

15th January

'First I was dying to finish high school and start college.
And then I was dying to finish college and start working.
And then I was dying to marry and have children.
And then I was dying for my children to grow old enough for school so I could return to work.
And then I was dying to retire.
And now, I am dying...and suddenly I realise I forgot to live.'

Anonymous

● ●

16th January

'If you have two diseases, the chances are that the second was caused by the treatment for the first.'

Vernon Coleman

● ●

17th January

'He who would be a man must be a non-conformist.'

Ralph Waldo Emmerson

• •

18th January

'There are no limitations to the mind except those we acknowledge.'

Napoleon Hill

• •

19th January

'Try to forget and forgive. If you can't do both then try to do one.'

Vernon Coleman

• •

20th January

'Your work is to discover your work, and then, with all your heart, to give yourself to it.'

Buddha

• •

21st January

'Information is the currency of democracy.'

Thomas Jefferson

• •

22nd January

'Dreams and memories are there to protect you from the dull and savage days.'

Vernon Coleman

• •

23rd January

'Tell the truth, and you are likely to be a pariah within your family, a semi-criminal to authorities and damned with faint praise by your peers. So why do we do it? Because saying what you think is the only freedom.'

Erica Jong

• •

24th January

'I find my spirits and my health affect each other reciprocally – that is to say, everything that discomposes my mind, produces a correspondent disorder in my body; and my bodily complaints are remarkably mitigated by those considerations that dissipate the clouds of mental chagrin.'

Tobias Smollett

• •

25th January

'Fashion is what one wears oneself. What is unfashionable is what other people wear.'

Oscar Wilde

• •

26th January

'The best, simplest and least asked question in the world is "Why?" Why do you want a better job? Why do you want to save money? Why do you want to move house? Why do you want to buy a holiday home? Only when you ask yourself "Why?" will you know what you really need and what you are prepared to do for it. Most people earn and spend without ever asking themselves "Why?" They blindly sell their time (which is the same as selling their lives) for money which they spend on things they neither want nor need. Ask yourself "Why?" more often and you will learn more about yourself and about what you are doing.'

Vernon Coleman

• •

27th January

'You must live as you think. If not, sooner or later you end up by thinking as you have lived.'

Paul Valery

• •

28th January

'A great healer heals with only a minimum of medicines. The superior healer knows how to heal the mind first. Even without any medicine.'

Tao Te Jing by Lao Tsu

• •

29th January

'The purpose of life is to know oneself. We cannot do it unless we identify ourselves with all that lives.'

Gandhi

. . . .

30th January

'The money required to provide adequate food, water, education, health and housing for everyone in the world has been estimated at $17 billion a year. It is a huge sum of money... about as much as the world spends on arms every two weeks.'

Dr Leo Rebello

. . . .

31st January

'When an archer misses the mark, he turns and looks for the fault within himself. Failure to hit the bull's eye is never the fault of the target. To improve yourself – improve your aim.'

Gilbert Arland

. . . .

1st February

'He who knows he has enough is rich.'

Tao Te Jing by Lao Tsu

. . . .

2nd February

'An Englishman in a state of adultery is miserable; even at the supreme moment his conscience torments him.'

Hippolyte Taine

• •

3rd February

'It is part of the cure to wish to be cured.'

Seneca

• •

4th February

'The invalid who takes a strenuous and indestructible interest in everything and everybody but himself, and to whom a dull moment is an unknown thing and an impossibility, is a formidable adversary for disease and a hard invalid to vanquish.'

Mark Twain

• •

5th February

'If you really want something then you must believe in your ability to get it. If you think you're going to fail then you'll almost certainly fail. If you think you can succeed then you'll stand a chance of succeeding.'

Vernon Coleman

• •

6th February

'We have to learn to become better ancestors.'

Jonas Salk

• •

7th February

'The natural force within each of us is the greatest healer of all.'

Hippocrates

• •

8th February

'All men are anarchists at heart, or, if they're not, they should be ashamed of themselves. To one and all of us, at some time or other, amid technocratic pressures and totalitarian intimations, must come the urge to kick over the orthodox traces, to say insultingly what we think, to reduce authority to the shambles it deserves.'

Michael Foot

• •

9th February

'I have a new philosophy. I'm only going to dread one day at a time.'

Charles M Schulz

• •

10th February

'There are only two truly infinite things: the universe and stupidity. And I am unsure about the universe.'

Albert Einstein

• •

11th February

'Virginity is like a balloon. One prick and it's gone.'

Vernon Coleman

• •

12th February

'Le germe n'est rien, c'est le terrain qui est tout.' ('The microbe is nothing, the soil is everything.')

Louis Pasteur

• •

13th February

'Time is the only little fragment of eternity that belongs to man; and, like life, it can never be recalled.'

Samuel Smiles

• •

14th February

'You have to know what you want to get it.'

Gertrude Stein

• •

15th February

'Smile! People will wonder why.'

Harry D Schultz

• •

16th February

'Cherish your youthful fantasies and enjoy them to the full. In a few years time all your waking hours will be spent worrying about mortgage rates, blocked drains and German measles.'

Vernon Coleman

• •

17th February

'If thou really desirest and would bravely find knowledge, open thine ears willingly to all men's views; have ability to study and comprehend their scope, and the will, courage and honesty to follow truth at all times, and however at first distasteful and unpopular.'

Confucius

• •

18th February

'You must come again when you have less time.'

Walter Sickert

• •

19th February

'Man is the only animal that blushes. Or needs to.'
  Mark Twain

• •

20th February

'The voice of conscience is so delicate that it is easy to stifle it; but it is also so clear that is is impossible to mistake it.'
  Madame de Stael

• •

21st February

'I am still waiting for something really wonderful to happen.'
  Woman celebrating her 100th birthday

• •

22nd February

'More people are made miserable trying to get rich – and failing – than are made happy by trying to get rich – and succeeding.'
  Vernon Coleman

• •

23rd February

'I couldn't take all those nut cases any more. You'd think once in a while somebody would notice that I have problems too.'
  Psychiatrist who shot a woman patient who kept ranting about her sex life

• •

24th February

'Man is quite insane. He wouldn't know how to create a maggot, and he creates Gods by the dozen.'

Michel de Montaigne

• •

25th February

'Lord, give me the courage to change the things which can and ought to be changed, the serenity to accept the things which cannot be changed, and the wisdom to know the difference.'

Alcoholics Anonymous prayer

• •

26th February

'I love everything that's old; old friends, old times, old manners, old books, old wines.'

Oliver Goldsmith

• •

27 February

'You have to be a friend to have friends. And true friendships take time to mature. Like seeds growing in the garden you can't hurry friendships; you have to let them take root, you have to be patient and attentive. Real wealth is measured in friendships – not material possessions.'

Vernon Coleman

• •

28th February

'The first half of our life is ruined by our parents and the second half by our children.'

Clarence Darrow

• •

1st March

'History is not what happened, it is what you can remember.'

W C Sellar and R J Yateman

• •

2nd March

'I am convinced digestion is the great secret of life.'

Sydney Smith

• •

3rd March

'Blessed is he who expects nothing, for he shall never be disappointed.'

Alexander Pope

• •

4th March

'Apologising for your mistakes is a sign of maturity and strength. Learning from your mistakes is a sign of true wisdom.'

Vernon Coleman

• •

5th March

'If you don't take chances you'll never know what would have happened. And you will always wonder. And always regret. Getting old and never knowing what might have been is almost certainly worse than getting old and having regrets. When you are old your regrets will tell you more about yourself than your accomplishments.'

Vernon Coleman

• •

6th March

'A man who moralises is usually a hypocrite, and a woman who moralises is invariably plain.'

Oscar Wilde

• •

7th March

'To constitute the millionth part of a legislature, by voting for one or two men once in three or five years, however conscientiously this duty may be performed, can exercise but little active influence upon any man's life and character.'

Samuel Smiles

• •

8th March

'An asylum for the sane would be empty in America.'

George Bernard Shaw

• •

9th March

'Old age is always 15 years older than I am.'

Bernard Baruch

• •

10th March

'Saying "I don't know" is a sign of strength not weakness.'

Vernon Coleman

• •

11th March

'If it weren't for the optimist, the pessimist would never know how happy he isn't.'

Anon

• •

12th March

'They cannot take away our self respect if we do not give it to them.'

Gandhi

• •

13th March

'When a man wants to murder a tiger he calls it sport; when a tiger wants to murder him, he calls it ferocity.'

George Bernard Shaw

• •

14th March

'Confront your fears and face the worst; it is the unknown which creates the monsters which will engulf you.'

Vernon Coleman

• •

15th March

'If you obey all the rules, you miss all the fun.'

Katharine Hepburn

• •

16th March

'Failure in any good cause is honourable, whilst success in any bad cause is merely infamous.'

Samuel Smiles

• •

17th March

'Life is simply one damned thing after another.'

Elbert Hubbard

• •

18th March

'I'm not for suppressing pornography. I'm for suppressing guns. Some pornography insults women, but none of it is as dangerous as the guns that kill women and men.'

Betty Friedan

• •

19th March

'I don't have ulcers; I give them.'

Harry Cohn

• •

20th March

'What is life but a series of sharp corners, round each of which fate lies in wait for us with a stuffed eelskin?'

P G Wodehouse

• •

21st March

'An after-dinner speech should be just like a lady's dress; long enough to cover the subject and short enough to be interesting.'

Anon

• •

22nd March

'I long ago came to the conclusion that it was horribly evil to experiment on other living beings and then attempt to justify the practice by calling it medical research.'

Sir John Gielgud

• •

23rd March

'He squandered health in search of wealth, to gold became a slave; then spent his wealth in search of health, but only found a grave.'

Message on a gravestone

• •

24th March

'Your body knows best. Learn to listen to it.'

Vernon Coleman

• •

25th March

'I'm just trying to get my life back together.'

Benjamin Petrosius, six-year-old actor

• •

26th March

'Sex is one of the nine reasons for reincarnation the other eight are unimportant.'

Henry Miller

• •

27th March

'Much of the world's work is done by men who do not feel quite well.'

J K Galbraith

• •

28th March

'In youth we tend to look forward; in old age we tend to look back; in middle age we tend to look worried.'

Anon

• •

29th March

'It doesn't matter what you do for a living. What matters is how proud you are of what you do.'

Vernon Coleman

• •

30th March

'The graveyards are full of indispensable men.'

Charles de Gaulle

• •

31st March

'The ultimate indignity is to be given a bedpan by a stranger who calls you by your first name.'

Maggie Kuhn

• •

1st April

'The best part of every man's education, is that which he gives to himself.'

Sir Walter Scott

• •

2nd April

'We don't hold much with talking to patients in this ward.'

A nurse

• •

3rd April

'I have known more men destroyed by the desire to have a wife and child and to keep them in comfort than I have seen destroyed by drink and harlots.'

W B Yeats

•••

4th April

'I am in favour of animal rights as well as human rights. That is the way of a whole human being.'

Abraham Lincoln

•••

5th April

'Obscene is not the picture of a naked woman exposed but that of a fully-clad general who exposes his medals won in a war of aggression.'

Herbert Marcuse

•••

6th April

'When you have difficulty saying "no" think of how much more difficult things are likely to become if you say "yes".'

Vernon Coleman

•••

7th April

'Chastity is the most unnatural of all the sexual perversions.'

Anon

•••

8th April

'Work is the refuge of people who have nothing better to do.'

Oscar Wilde

• •

9th April

'The more you know about yourself – and the more purpose your life has – the stronger you will become.'

Vernon Coleman

• •

10th April

'Well, this is a fine state of affairs, you damned desperado! You meet my son just as he comes out of the gymnasium, all fresh from the bath, and you don't kiss him, you don't hug him, you don't feel his balls! And you're supposed to be a friend of ours!'

Aristophanes

• •

11th April

'Money is the string with which a sardonic destiny directs the motions of its puppets.'

Somerset Maugham

• •

12th April

'Too bad all the people who know how to run the country are busy driving taxicabs and cutting hair.'

George Burns

• •

13th April

'If you are poor, and married to the woman you love everything becomes an adventure. A new hat for her is an achievement. The dreams, the plans, the obstacles that must be surmounted – the rich don't have any of that. There can be no castles in the air for people who live in castles.'

P G Wodehouse

• •

14th April

'Things which matter most must never be at the mercy of things which matter least.'

Goethe

• •

15th April

'Live your life honestly and with good intentions and you will enjoy the comfort of a clear conscience; now probably the only quality asset in a harsh, cruel world.'

Vernon Coleman

• •

16th April

'You have just dined, and however scrupulously the slaughterhouse is concealed in the graceful distance of miles, there is complicity.'

Ralph Waldo Emerson

• •

17th April

'Not only is love a source of delight, but its absence is a source of pain. Love is to be valued because it enhances all the best pleasures, such as music, and sunrise in mountains, and the sea under the full moon. A man who has never enjoyed beautiful things in the company of a woman whom he loved has not experienced to the full the magic power of which such things are capable.'

Bertrand Russell

18th April

'The man who is pulling his own weight never has time to throw it around.'

Peggy J Rudd

19th April

'Dying is a very dull, dreary affair. And my advice to you is to have nothing whatever to do with it.'

Somerset Maugham on his death bed

20th April

'If I had to live my life again, I'd make all the same mistakes – only sooner.'

Tallulah Bankhead

21st April

'One single book can significantly change the reader's attitude and action to an extent unmatched by the effect of any other single medium.'

Central Intelligence Agency (USA)

• •

22nd April

'When official spokesmen speak, you should only ever believe their denials. When official spokesmen deny something you can be confident that it is the truth.'

Vernon Coleman

• •

23rd April

'Roughly speaking there is about ten times more chance of being admitted to a mental hospital in any First World country than of being admitted to a university.'

R D Laing

• •

24th April

'Looks are so deceptive that people should be done up like food packages, with the ingredients clearly labelled.'

Helen Hudson

• •

25th April

'When you are getting kicked from the rear it means you are in front.'

Fulton J Sheen

• •

26th April

'If Michaelangelo had been straight, the Sistine Chapel would have been wallpapered.'

Robin Tyle

• •

27th April

'There are very few people who don't become more interesting when they stop talking.'

Mary Lowry

• •

28th April

'Everything great in the world comes from neurotics.'

Marcel Proust

• •

29th April

'In almost every society, pornography is reckoned as an offence, except when it is part of a religious ceremony.'

Bertrand Russell

• •

30th April

'Your only duty on this earth is to find yourself and live accordingly.'

Carl Jung

• •

1st May

'Success is truly the result of good judgement. Good judgement is the result of experience and experience is often the result of bad judgement.'

Anthony Robbins

• •

2nd May

'The sad lesson we learn from history is that hardly anyone ever learns anything from history.'

Robert Beckman

• •

3rd May

'A wise man ought to realise that health is his most valuable possession.'

Hippocrates

• •

4th May

'Year by year we are becoming better equipped to accomplish the things we are striving for. But what are we striving for?'

Dr Lawrence Peter

• •

5th May

'The more I see of people, the more I love my dog.'
   Samuel Pepys

• •

6th May

'All that is necessary for the triumph of evil is that good men do nothing.'
   Edmund Burke

• •

7th May

'Expecting the world to treat you fairly because you're a good person is like expecting a bull not to charge you because you're vegetarian.'
   Rabbi Mordechai Kaplan

• •

8th May

'You must laugh and be cheerful ten times a day or your stomach, that father of affliction, will disturb you in the night.'
   Frederich Nietzsche

• •

9th May

'Do not forget those who fought the battles for you, and bought your freedom with their genius and their blood.'
   Emile Zola

• •

10th May

'When I was young, I kissed my first woman and smoked my first cigarette on the same day. Believe me, never since have I wasted so much time on tobacco.'

Arturo Toscanini

• •

11th May

'To know that you do not know is the best. To pretend to know when you do not know is a disease.'

Tao Te Jing by Lao Tsu

• •

12th May

'Time is worth much more than money, so don't waste it – your own or anyone else's.'

Asa Baber

• •

13th May

'To be without some of the things you want is an indispensable part of happiness.'

Bertrand Russell

• •

14th May

'I only took with me two valets and a cook.'

The Marechal de Biron, reporting his imprisonment in the Bastille in 1631

• •

15th May

'Ignorance is expensive.'
 Harry D Schultz

. . . .

16th May

'It is one of life's laws that as soon as one door closes another opens. But the tragedy is we look at the closed door and disregard the open one.'
 André Gide

. . . .

17th May

'I attribute my whole success in life to a rigid observance of a fundamental rule; never have yourself tattooed with any woman's name, not even her initials.'
 P G Wodehouse

. . . .

18th May

'Some of my elderly patients still enjoy good sex – although they can't always remember the names of their partners.'
 Sex expert

. . . .

19th May

'Guests are like fish – they go off after three days.'
 Alan Plater

. . . .

20th May

'It has been my experience that folks who have no vices have very few virtues.'

Abraham Lincoln

• •

21st May

'What does not kill me makes me stronger.'

Frederich Nietzsche

• •

22nd May

'Life is what happens to you when you're busy making other plans.'

John Lennon

• •

23rd May

'If my doctor told me I had only six minutes to live, I wouldn't brood, I'd type a little faster.'

Isaac Asimov

• •

24th May

'It's probably true that hard work never killed anyone, but I figure why take the chance?'

Ronald Reagan

• •

25th May

'There are some ideas worth fighting for, and if you become a completely frightened and servile employee, a safe player at all times, you will become bored with yourself.'

Asa Baber

• •

26th May

'Prostitution gives her an opportunity to meet people. It provides fresh air and wholesome exercise, and it keeps her out of trouble.'

Joseph Heller

• •

27th May

'If you must slander someone, don't speak it, but write it. Write it in the sand, near the water's edge.'

Napoleon Hill

• •

28th May

'Acting and streetwalking are the oldest professions in the world and both are ruined by amateurs.'

Alexander Woollcott

• •

29th May

'If you limit your actions in life to the things that nobody can possibly find fault with, you will not do much.'

Lewis Carroll

• •

30th May

'Be good to the people you know. Take care of them and they'll take care of you.'

Asa Baber

• •

31st May

'Be kind to animals. Don't eat them.'

George Bernard Shaw

• •

1st June

'We know what happens to people who stay in the middle of the road. They get run down.'

Aneurin Bevan

• •

2nd June

'Love does not consist of looking at each other, but in looking outward together in the same direction.'

Antoine de Saint-Exupery

• •

3rd June

'Self pity is easily the most destructive of the non-pharmaceutical narcotics; it is addictive, gives momentary pleasure and separates the victim from reality.'

John W Gardner

• •

4th June

'A wife is a servant with an attitude problem.'

South African husband

• •

5th June

'Half the useful work in the world consists of combating the harmful work.'

Bertrand Russell

• •

6th June

'If you were to believe all the bad things that were said about you, you might as well close up shop and go out of business.'

Abraham Lincoln

• •

7th June

'One soul inhabiting two bodies.'

Aristotle, on the meaning of friendship

• •

8th June

'The desire of the man is for the woman, but the desire of the woman is for the desire of the man.'

Samuel Taylor Coleridge

• •

9th June

'Before the Cherry Orchard was sold everybody was worried and upset, but as soon as it was all settled finally and once and for all, everybody calmed down, and felt quite cheerful.'

Anton Chekhov

• •

10th June

'Most people will believe anything that tells against someone they dislike or flatters their self-esteem.'

Hesketh Pearson

• •

11th June

'I am their leader; I must follow them.'

Bertolt Brecht

• •

12th June

'Bravery is a synonym for having absolutely no imagination.'

Vernon Coleman

• •

13th June

'I have from an early age abjured the use of meat and the time will come when men such as I will look upon the murder of animals as they now look upon the murder of men.'

Leonardo da Vinci

• •

14th June

'Governments change. The lies stay the same.'

Anon

• •

15th June

'Bureaucracies are the most evil of man's institutions, they enshrine the worst of us and bring low the best of us.'

John Le Carré

• •

16th June

'When a fool does evil work he forgets that he is lighting a fire wherein he must burn one day.'

Buddha

• •

17th June

'The world is a comedy to those that think, a tragedy to those that feel.'

Horace Walpole

• •

18th June

'And she had suffered many things of many physicians, and had spent all that she had, and was nothing bettered, but rather grew worse.'

The Bible

• •

19th June

'The best man for the job is often a woman.'

Anonymous

• •

20th June

'You can't control the length of your life but you can control its width and depth.'

Tom Anderson

• •

21st June

'One half of the world cannot understand the pleasures of the other.'

Jane Austin

• •

22nd June

'The best armour is to keep out of range.'

Anonymous

• •

23rd June

'When a true genius appears in the world, you may know him by this sign, that the dunces are all in confederacy against him.'

Jonathan Swift

• •

24th June

'To animals belongs innocence.'

Frederich Nietzsche

• •

25th June

'It is the weak who are cruel. Gentleness can only be expected from the strong.'

Leo Roskin

• •

26th June

'An honest man is always in trouble.'

Vernon Coleman

• •

27th June

'The people who get on in this world are the people who get up and look for the circumstances they want, and if they can't find them, make them.'

George Bernard Shaw

• •

28th June

'Don't go around saying the world owes you a living, the world owes you nothing; it was here first.'

Mark Twain

• •

29th June

'Never give in. Never. Never. Never. Never.'
  Winston Churchill

• •

30th June

'Happiness? A good cigar, a good meal, and a good woman – or a bad woman. It depends on how much happiness you can handle.'
  George Burns

• •

1st July

'The Americans, like the English, probably make love worse than any other race.'
  Walt Whitman

• •

2nd July

'A loving wife will do anything for her husband except stop criticising and trying to improve him.'
  J B Priestley

• •

3rd July

'Children suck the mother when they are young and the father when they are grown.'
  John Ray

• •

4th July

'When I was a young man I observed that nine out of ten things I did were failures. I didn't want to be a failure so I did ten times more work.'

George Bernard Shaw

• •

5th July

'Life's under no obligation to give us what we expect.'

Margaret Mitchell

• •

6th July

'Nothing weighs less than a promise.'

Anonymous

• •

7th July

'The state does nothing except to assist the strong to despoil the weak.'

Clarence S Darrow

• •

8th July

'Loneliness and the feeling of being unwanted is the most terrible poverty.'

Mother Teresa

• •

9th July

'Old age isn't so bad compared to the alternative.'

George Burns

• •

10th July

'When men feel protective towards pretty women, they usually want to protect them against other (bad) men so that they can have a chance of doing to them what the bad men wanted to do.'

Godfrey D Fortune

• •

11th July

'May you live in interesting times.'

Chinese curse

• •

12th July

'He who laughs last hasn't much of a sense of humour.'

Vernon Coleman

• •

13th July

'Love is the delightful interval between meeting a beautiful girl and discovering that she looks like a haddock.'

John Barrymore

• •

14th July

'Victories are always temporary; so are defeats.'

   Mafia boss

• •

15th July

'There is hardly anyone whose sexual life, if it were broadcast, would not fill the world at large with surprise and horror.'

   W Somerset Maugham

• •

16th July

'The best way to avoid criticism is to keep quiet and do nothing. But what sort of life is that?'

   Vernon Coleman

• •

17th July

'Love is being stupid together.'

   Paul Valery

• •

18th July

'No-one can make you feel inferior without your consent.'

   Eleanor Roosevelt

• •

19th July

'Hunger is the best sauce in the world.'

Miguel Cervantes

• •

20th July

'All my possessions for a moment of time.'

Last words of Queen Elizabeth 1

• •

21st July

'This suspense is terrible. I hope it will last.'

Oscar Wilde

• •

22nd July

'All things tremble before danger, all fear death. When a man considers this, he does not kill or cause to kill.'

Buddha

• •

23rd July

'It's better that your enemies think you are crazy than reasonable and rational.'

Mafia boss

• •

24th July

'If you have men who exclude any of God's creatures from the shelter of compassion and pity, you will have men who will deal likewise with their fellow men.'

Jesus Christ

• •

25th July

'There are three things I always forget; names, faces and I can't remember the other.'

Italo Svevo

• •

26th July

'The old believe everything; the middle aged suspect everything; the young know everything.'

Oscar Wilde

• •

27th July

'Insanity in individuals is something rare – but in groups, parties, nations and epochs it is the rule.'

Frederich Nietzsche

• •

28th July

'No man can wear one face to himself and another to the multitude without finally getting bewildered as to which may be true.'

Nathaniel Hawthorne

• •

29th July

'Writing is an act of love. If not, it is merely paperwork.'

Jean Cocteau

• •

30th July

'With the exception of death the bottom line is hardly ever as bad as you think it's going to be.'

Vernon Coleman

• •

31st July

'During times of universal deceit, telling the truth becomes a revolutionary act.'

George Orwell

• •

1st August

'We should all do what in the long run gives us joy, even if it is only picking grapes or sorting the laundry.'

E B White

• •

2nd August

'A bargain is something you have to find a use for once you have bought it.'

Benjamin Franklin

• •

3rd August

'I always pass on good advice. It is the only thing to do with it. It is never of any use to oneself.'

Oscar Wilde

• •

4th August

'We must believe in luck. For how else can we explain the success of those we don't like.'

Jean Cocteau

• •

5th August

'Money is a good thing to have. It frees you from doing things you dislike. I dislike doing nearly everything so money is handy.'

Groucho Marx

• •

6th August

'Ninety-nine per cent of lawyers give the rest a bad name.'

Bumper sticker

• •

7th August

'A good laugh is a mighty good thing, and rather too scarce a good thing; more's the pity.'

Herman Melville.

• •

8th August

'If a man owns land, the land owns him.'

Ralph Waldo Emerson

• •

9th August

'We are part of the earth and it is part of us. The perfumed flowers are our sisters; the deer, the horse, the great eagle, these are our brothers.'

Red Indian leader Chief Seatlh

• •

10th August

'To get back my youth I would do anything in the world except take exercise, get up early or be respectable.'

Oscar Wilde

• •

11th August

'Women to me are like elephants. I like to look at them but I wouldn't want to own one.'

W C Fields

• •

12th August

'Nothing can harm a good man, either in life or after death.'

Socrates

• •

13th August

'God created woman. And boredom did indeed cease from that moment.'

Frederich Nietzsche

• •

14th August

'Of course, truth is stranger than fiction. Fiction has to make sense.'

Mark Twain

• •

15th August

'Look after the minutes as carefully as you look after the pennies and the hours, like the pounds, will look after themselves.'

Vernon Coleman

• •

16th August

'The treatment with poison medicines, comes from the West.'

Huang Ti, Chinese Emperor 2697 – 2597BC

• •

17th August

'Study sickness while you are well.'

Thomas Fuller

• •

18th August

'Men do not desire to be rich, only to be richer than other men.'

John Stuart Mill

• •

19th August

'We know for certain only when we know little. With knowledge, doubt increases.'

Goethe

• •

20th August

'Do not let a man practise to those beneath him that which he dislikes in those above him.'

Confucius

• •

21st August

'Never before have we had so little time in which to do so much.'

Franklin D Roosevelt

• •

22nd August

'I don't know what London's coming to – the higher the building the lower the morals.'

Noel Coward

• •

23rd August

'I don't want any yes-men around me. I want everybody to tell me the truth, even if it costs them their jobs.'

Samuel Goldwyn

• •

24th August

'I arise in the morning torn between a desire to improve (or save) the world and a desire to enjoy (or savour) the world. This makes it hard to plan the day.'

E B White

• •

25th August

'Nothing is terrible except fear itself.'

Francis Bacon

• •

26th August

'The tragedy of life is what dies inside a man while he lives.'

Albert Einstein

• •

27th August

'My formula for living is quite simple. I get up in the morning and I go to bed at night. In between, I occupy myself as best I can.'

Cary Grant

• •

28th August

'No grand idea was ever born in a conference.'

F Scott Fitzgerald

• •

29th August

'A man who has not passed through the inferno of his passions has never overcome them.'

C G Jung

• •

30th August

'Man remains what he has always been; the cruellest of all the animals, and the most elaborately and fiendishly sensual.'

George Bernard Shaw

• •

31st August

'It is the confession, not the priest, that gives us absolution.'

Oscar Wilde

• •

1st September

'The great end of life is not knowledge but action.'

Thomas Huxley

• •

2nd September

'The main trouble with the world is that someone put the grown-ups in charge.'

Vernon Coleman

• •

3rd September

'I've had a wonderful evening, but this wasn't it.'

Groucho Marx

• •

4th September

'Knaves nowadays look so honest that honest folk are forced to look like knaves so as to be different.'

Oscar Wilde

• •

5th September

'Remember, friends, as you pass by, as you are now so once was I. As I am now, so you must be. Prepare yourself to follow me.'

18th Century epitaph

• •

6th September

'I don't want to achieve immortality through my work – I want to achieve it through not dying.'

Woody Allen

• •

7th September

'Compassion for animals is intimately connected with goodness of character; and it may be confidently asserted he who is cruel to animals cannot be a good man.'

Arthur Schopenhauer

• •

8th September

'The good thing about the future is that it comes one day at a time.'

Abraham Lincoln

• •

9th September

'Whatever you do to the least of my brethren you do to me.'

God

• •

10th September

'The road of excess leads to the palace of wisdom.'

William Blake

• •

11th September

'Consistency is the last refuge of the unimaginative.'

Oscar Wilde

• •

12th September

'Hate usually does more damage to the person doing the hating than to the object of their hatred.'

Vernon Coleman

• •

13th September

'Education; that which discloses to the wise and disguises from the foolish their lack of understanding.'

Ambrose Bierce

• •

14th September

'Whenever I'm caught between two evils, I take the one I've never tried.'

Mae West

• •

15th September

'The best way to have a good idea is to have lots of ideas.'

Linus Pauling

• •

16th September

'I sometimes think that God, in creating man, somewhat overestimated his ability.'

Oscar Wilde

• •

17th September

'Coincidence is God's way of remaining anonymous.'

Anon

• •

18th September

'The Queen is most anxious to enlist every one who can speak or write to join in checking this mad wicked folly of Women's Rights.'

Queen Victoria

• •

19th September

'When a wise scholar hears the Tao
He practises it diligently.
When a mediocre scholar hears the Tao
He waves between belief and disbelief.
When a worthless scholar hears the Tao
He laughs boisterously (and foolishly) at its wisdom.'

Tao Te Jing by Lao Tsu

• •

20th September

'Everyone knows that you can buy money with your time. But only the wisest realise that you can also buy time with your money. Time is the most important, most fundamental currency in the world; the only currency that really matters.'

Vernon Coleman

• •

21st September

'The mass of men serve the state not as men but as machines, with their bodies. They are the standing army and the jailers and the constables. In most cases there is no free exercise whatever of the judgement or of the moral sense; but they put themselves on a level with wood and earth and stones; and wooden men can perhaps be manufactured that will serve the purpose as well. Such command no more respect than men of straw or a lump of dirt.'

Henry David Thoreau

• •

22nd September

'We have not abolished slavery, we have nationalised it.'

Herbert Spencer

• •

23rd September

'The whole of society will have become a single office and a single factory with equality of work and equality of pay.'

V I Lenin

• •

24th September

'Democracy and socialism have nothing in common but one word; equality. But notice the difference; while democracy seeks equality in liberty, socialism seeks equality in restraint and servitude.'

d'Alexis de Tocqueville

• •

25th September

'We put too much faith in systems and look too little to men.'
  Benjamin Disraeli

• •

26th September

'The worth of a State, in the long run, is the worth of the individuals composing it.'
  John Stuart Mill

• •

27th September

'...raindrops and weeds have already brought about the destruction of many a proud building.'
  Frederich Nietzsche

• •

28th September

'The effect of socialist doctrine on Capitalist society is to produce a third thing, different from either of its two begetters – to wit, the Servile State.'
  Hilaire Belloc

• •

29th September

'Anything acquired without effort and without cost is generally unappreciated.'
  Napoleon Hill

• •

30th September

'The socialists believe in two things which are absolutely different and perhaps even contradictory; freedom and organisation.'

Elie Halevy

• •

1st October

'When trouble is sensed well in advance it can easily be remedied; if you wait for it to show itself any medicine will be too late because the disease will have become incurable. As the doctors say of a wasting disease, to start with it is easy to cure but difficult to diagnose; after a time, unless it has been diagnosed and treated at the outset, it becomes easy to diagnose but difficult to cure.'

Niccolo Machiavelli

• •

2nd October

'It is every day becoming more clearly understood that the function of Government is negative and restrictive, rather than positive and active.'

Samuel Smiles

• •

3rd October

'Of all writings I love only that which is written with blood. Write with blood; and you will discover that blood is spirit.'

Frederich Nietzsche

• •

4th October

'The longest journey starts with the first step.'
  Confucius

• •

5th October

'The value of legislation as an agent in human advancement has usually been much over-estimated.'
  Samuel Smiles

• •

6th October

'We were the first to assert that the more complicated the forms of civilisation, the more restricted the freedom of the individual must become.'
  Benito Mussolini

• •

7th October

'However good your life is it will be better if you smile and say thank you more often.'
  Vernon Coleman

• •

8th October

'When a woman behaves like a man, why doesn't she behave like a nice man?'
  Dame Edith Evans

• •

9th October

'Literary coteries have no vital contact with the life of the community, and such contact is necessary if men's feelings are to have the seriousness and depth within which both tragedy and true happiness proceed.'

Bertrand Russell

10th October

'All the complaints which are made of the world are unjust; I never knew a man of merit neglected; it was generally by his own fault that he failed of success.'

Dr Samuel Johnson

11th October

'Life is a checkerboard and the player opposite you is time...you are playing against a partner who will not tolerate indecision.'

Napoleon Hill

12th October

'In a country where the sole employer is the State, opposition means death by slow starvation. The old principle: who does not work shall not eat, has been replaced by a new one: who does not obey shall not eat.'

Leon Trotsky

13th October

'The finest opportunity ever given to the world was thrown away because the passion for equality made vain the hope for freedom.'

Lord Acton

• •

14th October

'Just look at these superfluous people. They vomit their bile and call it a newspaper.'

Frederich Nietzsche

• •

15th October

'Must the citizen ever for a moment, or in the least degree, resign his conscience to the legislator? Why has every man a conscience then? I think that we should be men first, and subjects afterwards. It is not desirable to cultivate a respect for the law, so much as for the right. The only obligation which I have the right to assume, is to do at any time what I think right. Law never made men a whit more just; and by means of their respect for it, even the well disposed are daily made the agents of injustice.'

Henry David Thoreau

• •

16th October

'No laws, however stringent, can make the idle industrious, the thriftless provident or the drunken sober.'

Samuel Smiles

• •

17th October

'The mass of men lead lives of quiet desperation.'

Henry David Thoreau

• •

18th October

'What people fear when they engage in the struggle is not that they will fail to get their breakfast next morning, but that they will fail to outshine their neighbours.'

Bertrand Russell

• •

19th October

'Those who would give up essential liberty to purchase a little temporary safety deserve neither liberty nor safety.'

Benjamin Franklin

• •

20th October

'Only when you know why you do things will you know whether they are worth doing.'

Vernon Coleman

• •

21st October

'One needs only to know the letters of the alphabet in order to learn everything that one wishes.'

Edmund Stone

• •

22nd October

'Between him who in battle has conquered thousands upon thousands of men, and him who has conquered himself, it is the latter who is the greater conqueror.'

Buddha

• •

23rd October

'Talk about modest merit being neglected, is too often a cant by which indolent and irresolute men seek to lay their want of success at the door of the public.'

Washington Irving

• •

24th October

'Certain things are indispensable to the happiness of most men, but these are simple things: food and shelter, health, love, successful work and the respect of one's own herd.'

Bertrand Russell

• •

25th October

'Opportunity has hair in front, behind she is bald; if you seize her by the forelock you may hold her, but, if suffered to escape, not Jupiter himself can catch her again.'

Latin proverb

• •

26th October

'I learned grammar when I was a private soldier on the pay of sixpence a day. The edge of my berth, or that of my guard bed was my seat to study in; my knapsack was my bookcase; a bit of board lying on my lap was my writing table; and the task did not demand anything like a year of my life. I had no money to purchase candle or oil; in winter time it was rarely that I could get any evening light but that of the fire, and only my turn even of that. And if I, under such circumstances, and without parent or friend to advise or encourage me, accomplished this undertaking, what excuse can there be for any youth, however poor, however pressed with business, or however circumstanced as to room or other conveniences?'

William Cobbett

• •

27th October

'In the dissipation of worldly treasure the frugality of the future may balance the extravagance of the past; but who can say: "I will take minutes from tomorrow to compensate for those I have lost today?".'

Jackson of Exeter

• •

28th October

'Do not fear death so much, but rather the inadequate life.'

Bertolt Brecht

• •

29th October

'Perception is more important than reality.'

Vernon Coleman

• •

30th October

'Every moment lost gives an opportunity for misfortune.'

Napoleon Bonaparte

• •

31st October

'Lost wealth may be replaced by industry, lost knowledge by study, lost health by temperance or medicine, but lost time is gone for ever.'

Samuel Smiles

• •

1st November

'He who cannot change the very fabric of his thought will never be able to change reality, and will never, therefore, make any progress.'

Anwat Sadat

• •

2nd November

'Any fool can make a rule – and every fool will mind it.'

Henry David Thoreau

• •

3rd November

'The longer I live the more I am certain that the great difference between men, between the feeble and the powerful, the great and the insignificant, is energy – invincible determination – a purpose once fixed, and then death or victory. That quality will do anything that can be done in this world; and no talents, no circumstances, no opportunities will make a two legged creature a Man without it.'

Fowell Buxton

• •

4th November

'However men choose to regard me, they cannot change my essential being, and for all their power and all their secret plots I shall continue, whatever they do, to be what I am in spite of them.'

Jean-Jacques Rousseau

• •

5th November

'My rule is, deliberately to consider, before I commence, whether the thing be practicable. If it be not practicable, I do not attempt it. If it be practicable, I can accomplish it if I give sufficient pains to it; and having begun, I never stop till the thing is done. To this rule I owe all my success.'

John Hunter

• •

6th November

'One should as a rule respect public opinion in so far as is necessary to avoid starvation and to keep out of prison, but anything that goes beyond this is voluntary submission to an unnecessary tyranny, and is likely to interfere with happiness in all kinds of ways.'

Bertrand Russell

• •

7th November

'Have we not all eternity to rest in.'

Arnauld

• •

8th November

'I put my sole trust in my own strength of body and soul.'

Old Norse saying

• •

9th November

'Bureaucracy is a great machine operated by pigmies.'

Honoré de Balzac

• •

10th November

'The truest wisdom is a resolute determination.'

Napoleon Bonaparte

• •

11th November

'When I started writing seriously, I made the major discovery of my life – that I am right and everybody else is wrong if they disagree with me. What a great thing to learn. Don't listen to anyone else, and always go your own way.'

Ray Bradbury

• •

12th November

'I think I could turn and live with animals, they are so placid and self contained,
I stand and look at them long and long.
They do not sweat and whine about their condition,
They do not lie awake in the dark and weep for their sins,
They do not make me sick discussing their duty to God,
Not one is dissatisfied, not one is demented with the mania of owning things,
Not one kneels to another, nor to his kind that lived thousands of years ago,
Not one is respectable or unhappy over the whole earth.'

Walt Whitman

• •

13th November

'The subconscious mind will translate into its physical equivalent a thought impulse of a negative or destructive nature just as readily as it will act upon thought impulses of a positive or constructive nature. This accounts for the strange phenomenon which so many millions of people experience, referred to as "misfortune" or "bad luck".'

Napoleon Hill

• •

14th November

'Elderly relatives who enjoy poor health are like nymphomaniacs in short, tight skirts. Both are difficult to satisfy and impossible to get into and out of motor cars.'

Vernon Coleman

• •

15th November

'I don't deserve this award, but I have arthritis and I don't deserve that, either. So I'll take it.'

Jack Benny

• •

16th November

'Any pleasure that does no harm to other people is to be valued.'

Bertrand Russell

• •

17th November

'It doesn't matter where you live – where you live is really in your head.'

Henry David Thoreau

• •

18th November

'Is there one whom difficulties dishearten – who bends to the storm? He will do little. Is there one who will conquer? That kind of man never fails.'

John Hunter

• •

19th Novemer

'I was rich, if not in money, in sunny hours and summer days, and spent them lavishly.'

Henry David Thoreau

• •

20th November

'It is because millions only ever concern themselves with the trivia – the best way to make a padded pelmet and three ways to eradicate moss from your lawn – that our world has become the obscenely barbaric place it is.'

Vernon Coleman

• •

21st November

'I believe in the power of desire backed by faith because I have seen this power lift men from lowly beginnings to places of power and wealth; I have seen it rob the grave of its victims; I have seen it serve as the medium by which men staged a comeback after having been defeated in a hundred different ways...'

Napoleon Hill

• •

22nd November

'There is no greater calamity than to underestimate the strength of your enemy. For to underestimate the strength of your enemy is to lose the war. Therefore, when opposing troops meet in battle, victory belongs to the strategic planner.'

Tao Te Jing by Lao Tsu

• •

23rd November

'There is nothing either good or bad, but thinking makes it so.'

William Shakespeare

• •

24th November

'This spending of the best part of one's life earning money in order to enjoy a questionable liberty during the least valuable part of it, reminds me of the Englishman who went to India to make a fortune first, in order that he might return to England and live the life of a poet.'

Henry David Thoreau

• •

25th November

'The control of the production of wealth is the control of human life itself.'

Hilaire Belloc

• •

26th November

'It is necessary to plan and to organise in order to get rich. Staying poor is very easy; poverty needs no plan.'

Napoleon Hill

• •

27th November

'Only when you have found something you are prepared to die for will you know what life is all about.'

Vernon Coleman

• •

28th November

'Poverty takes away so many means of doing good, and produces so much inability to resist evil, both natural and moral, that it is by all virtuous means to be avoided...Let it be your first care, then, not to be in any man's debt. Resolve not to be poor, whatever you have spend less. Poverty is a great enemy to human happiness; it certainly destroys liberty, and it makes some virtues impracticable and others extremely difficult.'

Dr Samuel Johnson

• •

29th November

'No man ever stood the lower in my estimation for having a patch in his clothes; yet I am sure that there is greater anxiety, commonly, to have fashionable, or at least clean and un-patched clothes, than to have a sound conscience.'

Henry David Thoreau

• •

30th November

'The battle of life is, in most cases, fought up hill...if there were no difficulties there would be no success; if there were nothing to struggle for, there would be nothing to be achieved...All experience of life, indeed, serves to prove that the impediments thrown in the way of human advancement may for the most part be overcome by steady good conduct, honest zeal, activity, perseverance, and above all by a determined resolution to surmount difficulties, and stand up manfully against misfortune.'

Samuel Smiles

• •

1st December

'Power may be defined as organised and intelligently directed knowledge.'

Napoleon Hill

• •

2nd December

'He who knows when he has got enough is rich.'

Tao Te Jing by Lao Tsu

• •

3rd December

'Either I will find a way or make one.'

Family crest with a pickaxe on it

• •

4th December

'The family of emotions gratitude, friendship, respect etc. on which a stable society is based lose their meaning when it comes to the nomads, whose social conditions have created a different spirit. It is absurd to expect gratitude from the Moors, as it would be absurd to condemn them for being ungrateful. The sentiment of gratitude in its European sense follows from a set of social conditions in which contacts and needs are permanent; a given nomadic tribe will have a very different need tomorrow from the one it has today.'

Antoine de Saint-Exupery

• •

5th December

'Not for to hide it in a hedge,
Nor for a train attendant,
But for the glorious privilege
Of being independent.'

Robert Burns on money

• •

6th December

'The barriers are not erected which can say to aspiring talents and industry: "Thus far and no farther".'

Ludwig van Beethoven

• •

7th December

'Fill your house with gold and jade,
And it can no longer be fully guarded.
If you set store by your riches and honour,
You will only reap a crop of calamities.'

Tao Te Jing by Lao Tsu

• •

8th December

'Patience is the finest and worthiest part of fortitude, and the rarest too...Patience lies at the root of all pleasures, as well as of all power. Hope herself ceases to be happiness when Impatience companions her.'

John Ruskin.

• •

9th December

'Animal are those unfortunate slaves and victims of the most brutal part of mankind.'

John Stuart Mill

• •

10th December

'Work is my chief pleasure.'

Mozart

• •

11th December

'Have few friends but those thou hast, grapple them to thy heart with hoops of steel.'

William Shakespeare

• •

12th December

'A non observant man goes through the forest and sees no firewood.'

Russian proverb

• •

13th December

'The world is disgracefully managed, one hardly knows to whom to complain.'

Ronald Firbank

• •

14th December

'The truth is that our race survived ignorance; it is our scientific genius that will do us in.'

Stephen Vizinczey

• •

15th December

'If you want a friend, you must also be willing to wage war for him: and to wage war, you must be capable of being an enemy.'

Frederich Nietzsche

• •

16th December

'A difficulty is a thing to be overcome.'

Lord Lyndhurst

• •

17th December

'Purpose is the touchstone of any accomplishment, large or small. A strong man can be defeated by a child who has a purpose.'

Napoleon Hill

• •

18th December

'The average man is more interested in a woman who is interested in him than he is in a woman with beautiful legs.'

Marlene Dietrich

• •

19th December

'Misfortune is next door to stupidity.'

Russian proverb

• •

20th December

'He who has a why to live can bear with almost any how.'

Nietzsche

• •

21st December

'The verb "to doctor" means "to adulterate".'

Vernon Coleman

• •

22nd December

'I am the master of my fate, I am the captain of my soul.'

William Henley

• •

23rd December

'Nothing in the world is softer and weaker than water.
But, for attacking the hard and strong, there is nothing like water.'

Tao Te Jing by Lao Tsu

• •

24th December

'The primary sex organ in both men and women is the brain.'
   Sydney Biddle Barrows

• •

25th December

'I find more and more that it is well to be on the side of the minority, since it is always the more intelligent.'
   Goethe

• •

26th December

'Follow the course opposite to custom and you will almost always do well.'
   Jean-Jacques Rousseau

• •

27th December

'You don't have to realise your dreams to benefit from them. But you do have to keep them alive.'
   Vernon Coleman

• •

28th December

'Everything happens to everybody sooner or later if there is time enough.'
   George Bernard Shaw

• •

29th December

'To be seventy years young is sometimes far more cheerful and hopeful than to be forty years old.'

Oliver Wendell Holmes

• •

30th December

'Whoever said money can't buy happiness didn't know where to shop.'

Gittel Hudnick

• •

31st December

'Impossible is a word only to be found in the dictionary of fools.'

Napoleon Bonaparte

• •

micro censn.
U may m abode
small Mgs — hair, days, music
Not at first = "liberton
became opposite.

(o synctus

Small Mgs Matter
= naturalism
(General)
Dogma dont move us
song do
[but ... H resignation?]
le SIGNdm

Never simply.
small SELLOUTS   pimping ... (dogs)
hair, dogs, music ...   fight
a cohort   female resignation or
complying (how —oh! how it might
our women are not attacks or women)
pimping, not to devolve become the Mgs,
to selling pant ... but ... of course
Again, 78/now. rasta/Gangsta.
None of my business?

is A new cascade
(worth = resignation / E90. even say
Myle, street moral, NOT any big a
book. No cascade, (Pink Floyd/Motor)
No one do most draw attention, be excuse
= men, or boys. Rockstar behav. We
Many a tv —— We. does of by Tv?
who dont have a tv? No gays. who —

For a catalogue of Vernon Coleman's books
please write to:

Publishing House
Trinity Place
Barnstaple
Devon EX32 9HJ
England

| Telephone | 01271 328892 |
| Fax | 01271 328768 |

Outside the UK:

| Telephone | +44 1271 328892 |
| Fax | +44 1271 328768 |

Or visit our websites:

www.vernoncoleman.com
www.lookingforapresent.com
www.makeyourselfbetter.net

~1 Brian Jones

(+3) ...

Could it be?
over Politics.
Rock = Sellout (literal)
Jos Cole rock... Folk
commerc vs album sla...
etc

2) SKINS

"decent" in real life

majors of 'strong women'

why sing along
why not ———
   segregation / defeat
recogniseble

3) "street walky"
no visible
who do you want to look / be

complexs of "fashion" due to
   others to 78 ish
   no 2 girls
      no ... the street
      no funk
         no groups (a ...)

4) dream